SIMC

SEVEN STARS

A CORNISH CHRISTMAS PLAY FOR VOICES

HAIRY BEAR BOOKS

Who is that child I see wandering, wandering
Down by the side of the quivering stream?
Why does he seem not to hear, though I call him?
Where does he come from and what is his name?
                                    – Charles Causley

Good job Father Christmas came... cos I never
had much from mum and dad

                                    – Lauren Headon

FOR

JACK, TOM & JESSIE

FIRST PUBLISHED BY HAIRY BEAR BOOKS 2006
HAIRY BEAR BOOKS IS AN IMPRINT OF
GISS 'ON BOOKS LINKINHORNE CORNWALL PL17 7NS
© HAIRY BEAR BOOKS 2006
ISBN-10 0-9552869-1-3
ISBN-13 978-0-9552869-1-9
COVER: CLIVE WAKFER
© CLIVE WAKFER 2006
DESIGN BY HAIRY BEAR

PRINTED IN CORNWALL BY HEADLAND PENZANCE

SEVEN STARS

☙ MIZZLE ❧

LITTLE ELI

Lucky Duck! Awww! Lucky Duck!

FIRST VOICE

Little Elijah Crocker crept to the end
of his bed early on Christmas morning
and found not one, but two parcels
wrapped up in holly-motifed paper at
the bottom of the old white pillowcase
he had hung there just hours before.

LITTLE ELI

Lucky Duck!

FIRST VOICE

Backalong, in those dog-dancing days
when the conspiracy of Christmas was
still in its infancy, Yuletide was an unre-
markable time of the year which consist-
ed of little more than a good dinner,
more drink than usual, and a song or two

at church or chapel with family and good friends. But this particular year was different. After fingering the packaging of his parcels for a few moments before unwrapping a gleaming red plastic torch and silver bicycle bell, Little Eli opened his bedroom curtains and saw an even better gift (if that were possible); the thickest mizzle anyone could ever remember had rolled, unheard, from off the sea during the night and completely enveloped the Hill of Wonder.

LITTLE ELI

That winter was already as cold as a quilkin, mind. And now we were marooned, as if nothing and no one existed beyond that silent wall of mist. And probably they didn't.

FIRST VOICE

Gasped Little Eli, one of seven children who roamed – and thought they owned – the Hill of Wonder, which looked down on the charmed-but-not-charming village of Muskegy. The others were Billy Ough, Davy Isaacs, Jack Tusser, Dicky Dido, Jimmy Jampot and Jacey Blimmer.

LITTLE ELI

There were four of us Crockers lived in that cottage of poor render under corrugated iron: Father Crocker, Mother Crocker, Granfer Crocker and me, Little Eli Crocker. And we laughed and fought and scruffed along like any other poor family in that muddled era between old times and the new age. It wasn't romantic, or rustic; it just *was*. Father was a busy man. When he was home, he could barely stop for a cup of warm tea – and never long enough for a yarn. Always doing. Fixing stuff, growing stuff. Schemeing. We called him Billy Whizz.

Unshakeably cheerful, he liked everything and everyone, but rarely spoke of
where he'd been or what he'd done. For
all we knew, when he left for work each
morning he could have been taking part
in some vital operation to save mankind,
like Ilya Kuryakin. He gave us few clues.

MOTHER

But there was always food on the
table, and a few shillings besides for
niceys.

FIRST VOICE

Said Mother.

LITTLE ELI

Mother had a collection of house
coats and never wore fewer than three
pairs of socks at all times. She cooked
and bustled and bustled and cooked, and
possessed the most generous of blood-
red lipsticked smiles. Some of the children in the village thought she was The

Queen herself. And probably she was. Granfer grummled. Not with intent, but by way of entertainment. Like the proper farmers of old, he could find fault with anything... and we'd test him.

BILLY OUGH

Like doves, do ee, Granfer?

FIRST VOICE

Asked Billy Ough, through his chewed woollen balaclava.

GRANFER

Too bleddy white. Not 'nough flesh on un to feed a babe.

LITTLE ELI

The more we grizzled, the better he grummled.

DAVY ISAACS

We children were free to come and go as we pleased, backalong.

FIRST VOICE

Said Davy Isaacs, the schoolmaster's

favourite punchbag – though he had several.

DAVY ISAACS

Glory days, when mothers would set us loose after breakfast, with a jam sandwich, a bottle of water, a kiss on the forehead, and...

MOTHERS

Come home 'fore dark, mind.

❧ Chuffa ❧

Little Eli

But Christmas was different.

Dicky Dido

Christmas was a time for family – the one day of the year when we were expected to stay indoors.

First Voice

Said Dicky Dido, like the mouse-child he was.

Jimmy Jampot

Indoors all day, mind...

First Voice

Said Jimmy Jampot, with more than a note of regret.

Jacey Blimmer

And be indulged, petted, tolerated or ignored in equal measure, as the carnival of relations and neighbours paraded through our front parlour and good room.

FIRST VOICE

Agreed Jacey Blimmer, adjusting her knickers for the umpteenth time that day and fishing out a crumpled bag of boilings to hand round.

BILLY OUGH

It was a time when fathers and uncles and older brothers idled, drinking brown ale from brown bottles, while mothers and grans and big sisters were never seen without their pinnies, sleeves rolled to the elbow, emerging from the kitchen shrouded in steam, garlanded with the scent of roasting fowl, dusted with flour, trays laden with festive fare.

FIRST VOICE

Yes, Christmas was different all right. And this Christmas was the differentest of all.

LITTLE ELI

'Ere, come and look at nothing. This mizzle's some thick, you. Can't see a thing out there.

FIRST VOICE

The strangest things could happen when mizzle descended. Entire fleets of fishing boats had been known to disappear and then pop up again days later in a wholly unexpected location; their crews, watching over sagging sails and idle Lister engines, having no recollection of moving at all. Women, who had spent all of their married lives being faithful to tedious husbands, woke up in the arms – and beds – of the men they ought to have married, but didn't. Hardnuts and bullies would be led home safely after being found curled up in shop doorways scritching like babbies, all lost and remorseful.

BILLY OUGH

And, the very worst of all, small children went wandering. Mothers would swear they had dozed off for no more than moments, but that when they stirred, there was their dear one – Gone!

LITTLE ELI

That's what happened to Little Chuffa. Two years old. No trouble to no one. Quiet as a ghost. Dressed in a clown suit for Christmas Day. And gone.

BILLY OUGH

Chuffa was Aunt Porthia's little boy. Chuffa shunned toys, preferring to play with a large cardboard box, where he spent all his days...

CHUFFA:

Imagining...

LITTLE ELI

There was a hole in the side of the box, into which Aunt Porthia would insert a straw so he could drink. A book would be propped up for him outside the makeshift den and he would peer at it through this small hole. Finding himself in the alien surroundings of our house one Christmas Day, and bereft of his box, Chuffa sought another.

FIRST VOICE

One of the many empty crates of Co-op *Sweet & Golden* sherry that had been purchased for the occasion.

LITTLE ELI

And crawled inside for a nap.

FIRST VOICE

No one had a clue where he'd got to.

BILLY OUGH

The adults all went mazed, and we children joined in the adventure, searching everywhere we could think of... especially the places we weren't normally allowed in.

FIRST VOICE

But we'll leave them to their hunt just now, and move on – or rather back – to all those Christmases of old...

LITTLE ELI

I'll take me new torch... just in case.

❧ Pop ❧

First Voice

All the Christmases roll down the carn like great granite boulders heaved off the side of the quarry, and they stop at a tumbly-down cottage of crumbling lime and cement wash, clothed in a protective cloud of mizzle so dense a boy needed his Woolworth's torch in his pocket at all times, lest he be lost forever. Groping my way into the land of grey, I fumble like a blind man until I hear the unmistakable sound of pop, bubbling up from below.

Little Eli

A few days before Christmas, Father would arrange rows of William Jolly's famous mineral water bottles along the narrow ledges that divided the static and moveable parts of the sash windows in our house. The window frames were so rotten and so draughty that the glass appeared to levitate, and it was never necessary to open them for ventilation even on the hottest days of summer. From October to April newspaper was jammed into the cracks to help keep out the cold. And when December arrived, Father would begin to appear each evening with boxes of bottles, the only time of the year he succumbed to boughten booze and boughten pop. Never one for what he considered unnecessary fripperies or fancies, baubles or fairy lights, the Jolly's bottles were Father's only concession to Christmas decorations. Lined up on the window, their colourful contents glowed in the late afternoon sunlight, bathing the rooms in...

JACEY BLIMMER

Cherryade red...

BILLY OUGH

Limeade green...

JIMMY JAMPOT

Strawberryade pink...

DAVY ISAACS

Cola brown...

JACEY BLIMMER

And Orangeade... er, orange.

FATHER

Jolly's!

LITTLE ELI

Father would announce, standing back to admire the display.

FATHER

It's Top of the Pops!

LITTLE ELI

The rest of the year, we children drank cordials made from elderflowers, brambles and sloes, blackberry vinegar for colds, and a daily teaspoon of fish liver oil.

JACEY BLIMMER

From real fish.

LITTLE ELI

To ward off all manner of ailments. And evil spirits, too.

DICKY DIDO

And it worked!

LITTLE ELI

Dammee, it worked all right, for there were no demons brave enough to enter our house.

DICKY DIDO

Only rats in the roof.

BILLY OUGH

And not even cod liver oil would shift they buggers.

LITTLE ELI

Mother and Father, in turn, drank highly dangerous and often explosive concoctions brewed from anything they could scrounge from the hedgerows and fields. We children spent countless spring and summer weekends and evenings gathering dandelions, nettles and cowslips, tearing our young hands on gorse in order to procure the precious coconutty petals, which bubbled away for week after autumnal week, before joining the legions of bottles and clay jars in rows, like a miniature terracotta army marching nowhere, covering the floors, shelves and sills, filling every available space in the house, piggeries, barns and linhay.

FIRST VOICE

But at Christmas, *Sweet & Golden* sherry was purchased, great bottles of the caramel-smelling liquor, which was quaffed with relish and offered to anyone who called.

LITTLE ELI

I remember old Callum McQueen...

FIRST VOICE

Muskegy's loquacious postman, who spent more time on his round than any gent of his calling, and consequently knew more of the village's intrigues than any proper woman could ever hope to.

LITTLE ELI

Arriving at noon, settling down with a tumbler of *Sweet & Golden* and not stirring from the settee until after dusk, his sack of undelivered Christmas mail cushioning his slumbering dreams.

MOTHER

You looked so peaceful, it seemed a shame to wake ee, dear.

LITTLE ELI

Mother said to the dreamy fellow as she smoothed his hair, brushed cat fur from his jacket and sent him on his way.

☙ Aunt Sophe ☙

LITTLE ELI

The thing we children looked forward to most of all about Christmas Day back then wasn't the presents.

DICKY DIDO

Except when there was a new bike with navy blue paintwork and cream tyres...

DAVY ISAACS

Or a wind-up robot with red revolving eyes...

JACEY BLIMMER

Or a K-Tel LP...

BILLY OUGH

Or one o' they yo-yos ...

DAVY ISAACS

Or a proper model traction engine that you could steam up and get whistlin' an' scare the cat with...

DICKY DIDO

All packed into the pillowcase at the end of the bed.

LITTLE ELI

Yeah, yeah, all right, apart from all they. Like I was saying, the thing we children looked forward to most about Christmas Day back then wasn't the presents, but the visitors: the family and friends who were sometimes never seen from one year to the next. We had no idea who some of them were, and some never said a word to us, simply giving the occasional wink or ruffling our hair with scratchy fingers.

FIRST VOICE

But whoever they were, all settled their various and varying rears down to the feast on anything they could find that resembled a seat; a large uncle on a squat stool, a tiny aunt on a stepladder, two or three small children perched precariously on a card table, a row of assorted adults on a low garden bench, only their heads, like coconuts on a shy, visible above the starched table cloth, which was spread like a mighty white wave rising and falling in peaks and troughs over the assortment of furniture it concealed beneath.

LITTLE ELI

Everyone we weren't actually related to–

CHUFFA

'Ere, 'ang on there. Remember me? Little Chuffa! I'm still lost!

FIRST VOICE

Don't you worry now, Chuffa, we'll get to you by and by. Go on Eli...

LITTLE ELI

Er, ess, where was I again? Oh ess.

Everyone we weren't actually related to, but was over a certain age, was always known as, and addressed as:

JACK TUSSER

Uncle.

FIRST VOICE

We wondered when you might wake up, Jack Tusser.

LITTLE ELI

Or...

JACK TUSSER

Aunt.

FIRST VOICE

Much obliged Jack, but don't overdo it my son.

JACK TUSSER

Perhaps I will just have another forty.

FIRST VOICE

Ah, yes, uncles and aunts.

LITTLE ELI

Uncles and aunts. The consequence

of this was that until we grew older and worked out some of the muddled relationships of those seated round the groaning Christmas table, we had absolutely no way of telling if Aunt Hepsebah was our mother's sister, if Aunt Winnie was our father's brother's wife, or if Uncle Archie and Aunt Kitty were simply a couple who had served our parents tea during their annual caravan holiday to Hayle Towans. Inevitably, our allegiances were not built along blood lines, but guided and steered by far deeper motives, such as quality of gifts, unwavering kindness and the ability to pass on a good yarn.

JACK TUSSER

The weirder the better.

LITTLE ELI

Auntie Sophe, Mother's sister, would always be there.

JACK TUSSER

Broad shouldered, and with great bosoms to match, Aunt Sophe was the avowed enemy of pomposity and insincere politeness. It was said that she could swear for half an hour without a break and without repeating herself and that she set up tent each year at Whitsun Fair over Redruth and people happily paid a shilling to hear her curse. Some of the primmer relatives did not approve of Sophe, and only remained civil to her...

PRIM RELATIVE

Because 'tes Christmas.

JACK TUSSER

As if that had anything to do with anything.

LITTLE ELI

But we children loved Aunt Sophe. We loved her for her earthy laugh, for her free spirit, but most of all for her gifts. They didn't come wrapped in holly-motifed paper...

JACK TUSSER

But were just as prickly, mind.

LITTLE ELI

What Sophe saved up for us was half a dozen or more words and phrases of such a disgusting nature that we closed our eyes.

DICKY DIDO

Though not our ears, mind.

LITTLE ELI

When she revealed them. Words like...

AUNT SOPHE

Foo-foo.

LITTLE ELI

And...

AUNT SOPHE

Ficky-fucky.

BILLY OUGH

And...

AUNT SOPHE

Rattle-ass.

JIMMY JAMPOT

And...

AUNT SOPHE

Shagster.

DAVY ISAACS

And insults like...

AUNT SOPHE

Ass like a turf rick.

DICKY DIDO

And...

AUNT SOPHE

Got a mouth scrawed up like a duck's
fert.

JACEY BLIMMER

And...

AUNT SOPHE

Can't tell tin from turd.

JACK TUSSER

And...

AUNT SOPHE

Like a fart in a fair.

LITTLE ELI

And...

AUNT SOPHE

Shit for brains.

LITTLE ELI

And dozens and dozens of other rud-
isms to fill a young boy's heart with pure
delight.

FIRST VOICE

Uncle Dingley, awash with *Sweet &
Golden*, would clasp her around the
shoulders and say...

UNCLE DINGLEY

Sophe m'dear, you'm as rough as a
badger's ass.

AUNT SOPHE

Rough I may be, Dingley.

FIRST VOICE

She'd reply, shaking free of him.

AUNT SOPHE

But I wouldn' 'ave you, not if your ass was dipped in diamonds. So don't touch what you can't afford.

FIRST VOICE

Uncle Artie hardly said a word to anyone, but beamed and saluted with hand or cap as if he was the most contented guest in the room. And probably he was. From the moment he squeezed his moleskin-clad rear into the battered brown leather armchair until he got up to leave, he would sit, glass in hand and grinning, occasionally reaching down to take a bottle of Mackeson from the floor, cracking the crown cap with his teeth and pouring the contents lovingly, before declaring in the most syrupy brogue ever spoken...

UNCLE ARTIE

I'm jus' goin' murder another friend o' mine.

FIRST VOICE

His voice had the effect of turning even the starchiest of aunts into weak, swooning idiots. And perhaps this almost total abstention from conversation was born of a knowledge that his vocal power was a thing to be used with care. Perhaps Uncle Artie's larynx was dangerous trade, best kept locked up behind a closed smile, like a shotgun in a padlocked cupboard, safely out of harm's way lest it blow some woman, defenceless to its charm, clean away.

LITTLE ELI

Then there was Auntie Zilla and Uncle Stoat who, after barely three months of married life, discovered they hated the very sight of each other. But rather than divorce, and thereby incur the disapproval of fellow chapel-goers, Auntie Zilla and Uncle Stoat divided their house into two – him upstairs and her down. Everything was separate: entrances, bathrooms, bedrooms and kitchens. It proved the perfect arrange-ment and they were said to greet each other like neighbours each morning, often walking to work side by side, jok-ing and chatting like old friends.

FIRST VOICE

And here comes Uncle Hank.

LITTLE ELI

Real name Gary.

FIRST VOICE

Who had thick, hairy sideboards almost to his chin and ran a second-hand shop in Redruth called...

DAVY ISAACS

Zephyr.

FIRST VOICE

Which sold items he deemed to be...

UNCLE HANK

Cooool.

FIRST VOICE

Such as...

JACEY BLIMMER

Formica furniture.

JIMMY JAMPOT

Astro lamps.

DAVY ISAACS

78rpm records that played from the inside out.

JACK TUSSER

And old, well-thumbed copies of *Parade* magazine.

FIRST VOICE

Hank played slap-bass for a band called...

UNCLE HANK

Herbert Sherbet And The Dib-Dabs.

FIRST VOICE

The Dib-Dabs majored on Gene Vincent covers. Hank addressed everyone in a slow, what he presumably imagined to be American mid-West drawl, though he was unable to disguise...

LITTLE ELI

And we children couldn't fathom why he'd want to...

FIRST VOICE

His unmistakable Troon roots. Hank greeted all women as...

UNCLE HANK

Ma'am.

FIRST VOICE

And girls as...

UNCLE HANK

Li'l lady.

FIRST VOICE

While all men, regardless of status, were addressed as...

UNCLE HANK

Pard.

FIRST VOICE

And boys as...

UNCLE HANK

Nipper.

FIRST VOICE

Hank had a younger brother, Adrian, who was lead singer for The Flying Fucks, Cornwall's first punk rock group, while at the same time playing second euphonium in the town band. A quiet sort of chap who worked behind the counter of Rowe's greengrocer's, Adrian saw no conflict of artistic interest in marching up Fore Street in uniform playing *The White Rose* on a Saturday afternoon and bawling out the lyrics of *Camborne To Be Wild*, *Road To Polruan* or *Like A Bat Out Of Hayle* at the Flamingo nightclub the same evening.

ADRIAN

Hell, 'tes all music, you.

FIRST VOICE

Adrian would say, trying to disguise a black eye under the peak of his town band cap.

ᴄᷓ A Geek ᷓᴄ

CHUFFA

Ahem, this is all very well and inter-
esting and that, but I haven't gone
nowhere. I'm still lost!

FIRST VOICE

Patience, Chuffa, patience. I want to
tell you about Uncle Lolly. Uncle Lolly
did taxidermy.

UNCLE LOLLY

Shrew or prize stallion, 'tes all the
same to me.

FIRST VOICE

And told tales of sea voyages.

UNCLE LOLLY

Oh ess, I seen monsters, all right.

FIRST VOICE

And of watching Cuban girls, dancing
naked.

UNCLE LOLLY

Aw man, you never seen the like, never seen the like.

LITTLE ELI

We children listened in rapt astonishment to it all, though of course we knew there wasn't an inch of truth in any of Uncle Lolly's yarns.

BILLY OUGH

It was the fact that he actually thought we believed him that was so unbelievable.

DAVY ISAACS

I mean, how could it be anything but lies?

DICKY DIDO

After all, we'd each paid sixpence to watch Belinda Strick strip off in the woods over Carnkie.

LITTLE ELI

She just stood there bare and

whistling *Hi Ho Silver Lining* for a full five minutes while we had a good geek.

BILLY OUGH

I mean to say, how could Uncle Lolly possibly get himself all lathered up about naked Cuban girls?

JACK TUSSER

Money would have been better spent on a couple of rides on the Waltzers over Redruth Fair.

FIRST VOICE

Then there was Aunt Pearl. The slightest little scrap of a woman you ever saw, she always wore the same thin, colourless cotton dress, through which poked the angular frame of a corset several times too big for her, the straps hanging off her shoulders, she rattling round inside like a rat in a barrel.

LITTLE ELI

Aunt Pearl never said nothing to no

one, unless forced to.

FIRST VOICE

Fidgety, frail and brittle, she held a secret few can believe even to this day. A letter, addressed to the family, was discovered in her room, after her body...

LITTLE ELI

All gashly white...

FIRST VOICE

Was found face down in a dew pond on the carn one bright April morning. In this letter, Aunt Pearl told her story. Though a spinster all her 54 years, it seems that she had dipped her toe...

JACK TUSSER

And a bit more besides, mind...

FIRST VOICE

Into the fast-flowing river of lust. A trader, whom she declined to name in her posthumous testament, had flattered her...

JACK TUSSER

And a bit more besides, mind...

FIRST VOICE

Without tenderness or love in the back of his van, before leaving her with far more than a grubby memory. Aunt Pearl was a seamstress, so when the scrap was born dead behind the Dutch barn after she had concealed the wretched lump beneath layers of jumpers for more than seven months, she took it to the quarry road, where she'd seen a dead badger lying a few days earlier. There, she deftly slit open the beast's gut, removed the entrails and replaced them with her poor, dead baby. She then stitched up the animal's stomach and placed it on the rough and bouldery track, over which she knew the stone lorries would rumble the following day. Their wheels pounded over both badger and babe until not a scrap of either remained.

JACK TUSSER

God struth man.

LITTLE ELI

One visitor who never missed Christmas Day in our house was Auntie Bessie Bubby. She would be the first to arrive and the last to leave, bustling continuously through the intervening hours. And she was a Godsend to Mother, much preferring scrubbing pans to socialising, scraping spuds to swigging sherry. Good job too, because few could understand much of what Auntie Bessie Bubby said when she did join in with a conversation. Issuing indecipherable colloquialisms, it is hard to believe fellow residents of her native Lancashire understood her any better than the bewildered souls of my village.

FIRST VOICE

Others also made their significant impression on these young minds.

BILLY OUGH

Aunt Mahala, in pigtail plaits, would pontificate on The Arts, stating that...

AUNT MAHALA

Anyone who says he doesn't like Shakespeare has the intellect of an ass and the imagination of my Bottom.

JACK TUSSER

Auntie Flossie, farting like a steer.

JACEY BLIMMER

Enormous Auntie Kay Cole, eating everything in sight, spearing leftover slabs of meat or pastry from the plates of other diners.

JIMMY JAMPOT

Boring Uncle Melville, who cycled between villages with a sturdy contraption strapped to his bicycle, regaling even the smallest niece about his latest triumph in the...

UNCLE MELVILLE

Gramophone contests.

FIRST VOICE

And many other strange and wonderful folk, their inhibitions loosened by drink and safe company.

ও PRAZE ও

LITTLE ELI

Grace was invariably said by Uncle
Silvanus, a beef farmer. Plunging a carv-
ing knife into the breast of the bird, he
would declare...

UNCLE SILVANUS

Without death there is not life.

FIRST VOICE

To which, the entire assembled multi-
tude would reply...

ALL

Rub-a-dub-dub and thanks for the
grub.

LITTLE ELI

Before the feast could begin, Uncle
Linnet would always say a prayer.

UNCLE LINNET

Let Us Pray. Let us Praa... Sands

ALL

Godolphin be with you!

UNCLE LINNET

Chyandour Trebartha

Looe art in St Keverne

Porthallow be thy Rame

Thy Kingsand Come-to-Good

Thy Withiel be Dunheved

In St Erth as it is in Porthleven

Geevor us St Day our Gribben Head

And Relubbus our Tresparretts

As we St Ive Trevose Gugh

Trespearne Relubbus

But Trelever us from St Eval

For Constantine is the Ding Dong

Pendower and the Cury

St Clether, St Clether

ALL

Land's End.

UNCLE LINNET

Praze-an-Beeble.

ALL

Stenalees be with you.

FIRST VOICE

After the meal, Uncle Denzil would sit on the settee all afternoon with soft and voluptuous Auntie Kay wriggling and giggling on his lap, all the time stroking his hair, petting him and whispering to him. Uncle Denzil would slap her great soft pookie ass and declare...

UNCLE DENZIL

If you want a happy marriage, boy, marry a happy woman.

LITTLE ELI

Invariably one uncle, who the grownups all called Jimmy Redass...

JACK TUSSER

Though they never would tell us why...

LITTLE ELI

Would stand up after tea each year,

without fail, his eyes still closed from sleepy over-indulgence, and recite:

JIMMY REDASS

I seduced a young woman
In a sycamore tree,
Or was it on a beech?
She lay back in arboreal rapture
And offered me a peach.
And as I climbed, like a scrumping lad,
That fruit I'd thought out of reach
Was gently placed beneath my lips
The loveliest lesson to teach.

LITTLE ELI

Before sinking back into armchair and stupor, his audience momentarily pausing from whatever they were doing, as one might watch a noisy jet fly overhead.

FIRST VOICE

Sufficiently revved up by Jimmy Redass, Uncle Clinker would follow, with a recitation of his favourite poem, *The Rhyme Of The Ancient Pedant*:

UNCLE CLINKER

I said, 'Dad, can we go to Launceston?'
He said, 'Of course we can, son.
We'll go via Crows an Wra,
It's quicker that way.
We'll pass through Breage,
It's not out of our league
And on to Caerhayes
It'll take us days.
Down to Fowey,
You'll like it there, boy,
We'll bypass Lewannick
Where the girls are platonic,
But go through to Illogan
For a nice piece o' fuggan.
Down to Liskeard,
Where we'll stress that we're 'ard
And insist on Redruth
Or become quite uncouth.

On to Philleigh
If you don't think that's silly,
And over Pennance
Where the folks look askance,
Then call in on Dennis
Up at St Gennys
And pop in on Steve
By lovely St Ive,
Then on to St Keyne
Just to say that you've been
And delight in St Eval
You lucky lil' devil.
We'll see Biscovey
On a nice sunny day,
Then arrive in Launceston
Where they'll know you're a
Cornish man, son.'

❧ GRUNT ❧

CHUFFA

Excuse me. I've about had enough of this. It's bleddy freezin' out 'ere. Will some bugger please hurry up and find me.

FIRST VOICE

Patience, Chuffa, patience!

LITTLE ELI

At Christmas, our little house creaked with the pressure of so much flesh, its furniture groaning under the weight of so many backsides. But this was nothing to the pressure brought to bear on the plumbing. We children peed pretty much free-range in those days and were never discouraged, for the more we used the hedges the less of a burden we put on the chemical toilet. Chemical toilet.

Hell! Those words still possess the power to conjure real loathing. The chemical toilet, that skulked in a corrugated iron shed in the corner of the yard, half covered in ivy like a veil of deceit, concealing the terrible pit that lurked behind the door, with its stiff latch and voracious insect life. It wasn't the smell that offended – if truth were told, the smell was faintly comforting, like red diesel, freshly mown grass, or the unmistakable garlicky whiff of cattle breath after they've been grazing on wild ramson – but the fear of what lurked beneath the murky surface of the vat, over which we perched on wooden slats and which, at any moment, as you sat there, even momentarily, might rise up from the depths, a mass of snapping teeth, and take off your boyhood in a single bite. I would rush from there, leaving the door swinging, clutching my shorts and making sure I was a safe distance away before buckling belt and buttoning flies. However, this terror and disgust didn't extend to every member the family; I once found Granny Grunt slumped in there, all brown-gusseted, her head lolling on one side. I thought she must be dead, for why else would anyone stay in there any longer than was absolutely necessary? But with the sight of a half-finished cup of tea, Thermos flask, bag of Mintoes and a copy of *The People's Friend* came the awful realisation that she had voluntarily chosen to imprison herself in that dungeon of disgust, which bore more resemblance to some medieval punishment cell than the 20th century porcelain conveniences enjoyed by my contemporaries. But there were benefits: tomato seeds, already conveniently manured as they passed through our digestive systems and spread on the back paddock, produced a fine crop which could be harvested throughout the summer. In particularly bountiful years we sold them from a table at the gate and it was always a joy to consider how passing holidaymakers might react if they knew the tortuous path these tomatoes had taken in order to grace their salads. This roadside stall could be quite lucrative, a special favourite being stone jars dug from the Victorian tip, filled with cheap-as-chips jam or tomato chutney from the Co-op and sold as home-made.

FIRST VOICE

Proof that the palate is a fickle friend; tell it it is being fed on Co-op budget strawberry and that is what it tastes, but tell it it is being graced by a preserve made with locally-grown fruit cooked to a traditional recipe and it will somersault into raptures of delight.

ᥩ IN TURD ᥩ

LITTLE ELI

Christmas was an odd time of year in many ways because, except for us lads–

JACEY BLIMMER

And a few of us younger maids...

LITTLE ELI

Everyone – adults that is – stayed indoors for days and days on end whatever the weather, wittering about the next meal and drowning in cheap sherry. As soon as the present-opening and figgy pudding ritual was over, we boys–

JACEY BLIMMER

And a few of us younger maids...

LITTLE ELI

Stole out into the mizzle, dressed against the dampness in uniform grey or khaki duffle coats.

DICKY DIDO

With real bone toggles.

LITTLE ELI

Or hooded green parkas.

DICKY DIDO

With real rabbit fur trim.

DAVY ISAACS

Jimmy Jampot had a navy gabardine mac.

DICKY DIDO

With a real plastic red key on a chain sewn into the pocket.

BILLY OUGH

He said he once used it as a weapon and had whirled it round his head.

JIMMY JAMPOT

Like a Hell's Angel!

BILLY OUGH

And scared off a whole gang of boys from over Tregajorran who'd transgressed an unwritten law by trespassing into our village.

DICKY DIDO

To beat up Grammar-sows.

DAVY ISAACS

We never said, but the rest of us knew, of course, having suffered a good kicking for freeing them Tregajorran boys' goat one time, that it would have taken more than a plastic red key to frighten they.

LITTLE ELI

At any other time of the year we might take our Hercules and Chopper bikes over Camborne.

DICKY DIDO

Where no one knew us.

LITTLE ELI

And cycle through Woolworth's or Lipton's or the International Stores.

BILLY OUGH

Or shoot Jimmy's air rifle at bottles.

DICKY DIDO

Or play cowboys and indians.

DAVY ISAACS

Or Stag-stag-stag.

LITTLE ELI

Sometimes we'd scour the quarry
pools for unsuspecting amphibians,
stuffing our saddlebags with jam jars full
of the unfortunate creatures and pedal
over Illogan.

DICKY DIDO

Where Froggy Skewes would give us a
penny a dozen.

LITTLE ELI

We collected them like other boys
collected shrews' skulls or Corona bottles, believing Froggy bred them and
kept them as pets.

BILLY OUGH

Truth was, they were either shipped
to France to be devoured in restaurants

or more likely ended up in some ghashly laboratory.

LITTLE ELI

Sometimes we'd roam the churchyard, reading the headstones, and creasing up and grizzling at the names.

ALL CHILDREN

In turd! In turd!

LITTLE ELI

We'd chorus.

ALL CHILDREN

Here lies Parson Pratt. In Turd!

LITTLE ELI

And we all chanted along with the mantra, doubled up with laughter.

LITTLE ELI

On fine days we might climb up to play among the ruins of an old village, which clung to a small quarry on the higher slopes of the Hill of Wonder. There were seven or eight little cottages in a row, all roofless and half of them no more than three granite courses high. On the end had been built a chapel, which was distinguished only by an arched window space but with no glass or frame remaining. Billy once found a broken china tea cup there, which had the embossed face of John Wesley himself on one side and the word...

BILLY OUGH

Primitive.

LITTLE ELI

On the other.

FIRST VOICE

This village, which had no name anyone could recall, though some referred to it as Rattle Row, had been a thriving little community, with even a narrow tramway, the granite sleepers still visible in places, leading to the base of the carn. Then...

LITTLE ELI

And our parents assured us it was a true story.

FIRST VOICE

One night there came such a wind as had never been heard before. It tore down great trees, lifted ellins like they were autumn leaves, smashed all the windows in the school and schoolhouse–

JACK TUSSER

I done that since, mind...

FIRST VOICE

Uprooted Cornish elms and generally terrified anyone who heard it.

LITTLE ELI

Not a drop of rain, just wind.

FIRST VOICE

The next morning, when the postman picked his way through the debris to Rattle Row, he found nothing but silence. Not a soul was there. Men, women, children, goats, bullocks, fowl, all gone.

LITTLE ELI

And they were never found.

FIRST VOICE

It seems the wind had simply entered their houses, picked them up, and lifted them into the heavens.

BILLY OUGH

One year, I watched rabbits in the thorn trees up Rattle Row. I swear I did.

LITTLE ELI

It was the only time we ever had proper snow. Great cotton wool waves of the stuff.

BILLY OUGH

And the rabbits were as surprised as me. See, what had happened was they'd scampered up the drifts on to low branches in search of food to nibble, and been left high and dry when the thaw

came. I ran and told anyone who was
about.

LITTLE ELI

We let all the rabbits down carefully
and watched them bound off.

BILLY OUGH

Never dared wring their necks and
take them home for tea that day, after
Jack said...

JACK TUSSER

They rabbits carry the souls of the
villagers who was blown away.

FIRST VOICE

But these were pastimes and distrac-
tions for every other season. At mizzley
Christmastime...

LITTLE ELI

We'd meet up to walk between invisible stone hedges, listening to an invisible
blackbird singing on an invisible branch,
and Ralph Finch's invisible dog...

JIMMY JAMPOT

Which was tethered, poor thing, even though it only had three legs...

LITTLE ELI

Barking in the distance. Then calling out for each other.

BILLY OUGH

'Ere Dicky, that you?

JACK TUSSER

Naw, 'tes a snowman.

LITTLE ELI

We would look for droplet-laden cobwebs on the furze, and wander the deserted lanes in search of people to grizzle at. At any other time of year there were plenty of candidates to choose from.

DAVY ISAACS

There was Cathy Cute, for a start, who lived in a tent over the back of the carn with her dad...

FIRST VOICE

Cute Behenna, a horse dealer...

DAVY ISAACS

And the scariest human being any of us had ever laid eyes on.

LITTLE ELI

She was a Behenna too, but no one ever called her anything other than Cathy Cute.

FIRST VOICE

He was called 'cute' on account of his cunning ways, so Cathy was branded for life with the same reputation. Cathy was dark-skinned – and very beautiful in later years. She was rarely seen without a tatty tartan tam o' shanter pulled down tight over her eyebrows, and she smelled strongly of smutties.

LITTLE ELI

We would tease her rotten, 'til she ran home to her dad, crying, to taunts of...

ALL CHILDREN

Smeechy-ass, smeechy-ass.

LITTLE ELI

We were nasty little buggers really, though I came to regret our treatment of Cathy Cute. It wasn't just that she refused to look at me when she'd flowered into the most exotic creature that ever walked the Hill of Wonder, but that her father caught me trying to start up his dump-truck one night, and beat the shit out of me. I had broken fingers, and lips bloodied and swollen like raw liver. He half killed me. And it wasn't for tampering with the truck, that's for sure, but stored-up retribution for all those years of tormenting his Cathy. Mother hardly recognised me. I said I'd fallen off the quarry. Mother cleaned me up, took me to the hospital, and when the doctors and nurses had finished with me and

made sure I'd live to tell the tale, she
took me home and slapped me sore.

MOTHER

For lyin'.

LITTLE ELI

And put me on jankers for a month.

DICKY DIDO

Then there was Mad Mick, who, if
you should so much as glance at him–

JACK TUSSER

Though staring worked better, mind...

DICKY DIDO

Would launch into a tirade of the
most incomprehensible gibberish.
Sometimes we might catch the odd
word, though Jack would never accept
that any of it was English and swore
blind Mad Mick had to be some kind
of...

JACK TUSSER

Incarnation.

DICKY DIDO

Muttering all manner of...

JACK TUSSER

Incantations.

DICKY DIDO

Whatever he was, and whatever he said, we would always end up running away, with him shouting after us...

MAD MICK

Doan tay de pid ouda me doo bouda, kiga fudn edn. Doan tay de pid ouda me doo bouda, kiga fudn edn.

FIRST VOICE

It wasn't until years later that they realised Mad Mick hadn't started out mad at all, but that his deafness had led to misunderstandings, which gave way to frustration and finally rage, leaving him...

ALL CHILDREN

Mad As Hell.

LITTLE ELI

He must have thought we were such cruel little buggers.

DICKY DIDO

And perhaps we were.

ಲ UGGIE ಲ

LITTLE ELI

We could spend a whole afternoon, at
other times of the year, perched like
starlings on the tin roof over Old Man
Clodgy's place, watching him try to
teach a new trick to Uggie, his ancient
Jack Russell terrier. Old Man Clodgy
would walk to one corner of the paddock, leaving Uggie, totally bewildered
and licking his behind, at the other.
Then he'd call him, in the hope that the
dog would respond in the time-honoured
fashion. Sometimes Uggie would do his
bit to humour the old man. Other times
he'd just roll over and sleep. But Clodgy
would just keep on hollering until he got
a response. And invariably the dog
would deliver.

CLODGY

Uggie! Uggie! Uggie!

UGGIE

Woof! Woof!Woof!

CLODGY

Uggie!

UGGIE

Woof!

CLODGY

Uggie!

UGGIE

Woof!

CLODGY

Uggie! Uggie! Uggie!

UGGIE

Woof! Woof!Woof!

LITTLE ELI

But our favourite was Hedley. We ragged him, though it was never malicious, and we loved him dearly. If other boys so much as looked at him funny...

JACK TUSSER

We'd lace 'em.

LITTLE ELI

Hedley always had time for us. And when he saw us coming, he'd set down his sack, recline on the pavement and adopt an expression of rapt expectancy, like a cat waiting to have its tummy tickled. Sometimes we'd have something to tell him, but more often it was Hedley who would do the telling.

HEDLEY

Schooldays. Never did me no harm. Never did me no good nuther, mind. Learned 'ow to get into scraps and out o' scrapes. But when it came to larnin' trade, I was gone. Gone like yes'day's clouds. Leggin' it down road, schoolmaster 'ollerin arter me. Naw, I thought I was far too smart for they. Thought they teachers cudden teach me nothing.

Truth was I dedn' knaw 'nough to knaw what I dedn' knaw, if you'm follerin' my meanin'. 'Course, having no larnin' – reading and writing trade – has its drawbacks. Cost me dear, especially in the early days. Oh ess, I've paid for my lack of attention in class. Ess, I paid for'n in giggles an' smirks from snickerin' schoolboys an' grizzlin' grannies.

FIRST VOICE

But the truth was that if it hadn't been for Hedley's total lack of interest in school, he might never have attained the status he finally achieved. For although to his mother he remained Hedley King, the rest of the world addressed him by the glorious title of...

LITTLE ELI

Hedley Headlines.

HEDLEY

Still, here I am, cog in the wheel, this

job keeps me busy, spreading the word, like. Something happen in this district, you can rely on ol' Hedley to tell the whole blimmin' neighbourhood.

FIRST VOICE

Hedley was the sole paperboy for the *Cornish Evening Tidings*. Each day at four o'clock on the dot he would pick up...

HEDLEY

Two 'undred brand fangin' new copies of the *Tidings*...

FIRST VOICE

Along with a large bill poster proclaiming to anyone interested the most pressing news of the day. As well as delivering, Hedley's job entailed shouting the contents of this bill from street to street, house to house.

LITTLE ELI

Only problem was Hedley couldn't read it.

HEDLEY

No bother there, says I, on my first day at the job, I'll jus' ask a edycated gent. 'What 'a say 'ere?' says I, pointing to the bill.

EDYCATED GENT

Why, 'Mayor Announces Election'.

HEDLEY

Says ee. 'Very good,' says I, thanking him and goes on my way, down Fore Street, proclaiming to all 'Mayor 'Nounces 'Lection' an' selling copies as I go. Tuppence a piece. So by the time I've walked down through the town, stopping for a yarn here and a roll of bacca there, up Station Hill and over Green Lane, down Trewirgie and back to Sandy Lane, my sack is considerably lighter and my money pouch considerably heavier. Very smooth. Nex' day, same story... only defferent, like, on account of the news changin' all the time.

FIRST VOICE

And so it went on, Hedley's employer being very happy and Hedley himself making a bit of a name for himself in the town on account of him being able to holler louder than any previous paper seller.

HEDLEY

After 'bout a week, mind, I'm just coming out with my bundle o' papers, a g'eat grin across me chacks, proud as a peacock, though I can't think why, when who should I see but young Bazooka Joe.

FIRST VOICE

Now Bazooka was a bit of a rascal – and him from a Temperance family too.

HEDLEY

I knaw ee 'ad the readin' so I ups and says: 'Ere, what 'a say 'ere?'

BAZOOKA JOE

Eh?

HEDLEY

Says ee, acting like ee's daft or somethen. 'What 'a say on this g'eat bill 'ere?'

BAZOOKA JOE

Aww...

HEDLEY

Says ee slowly, beginning to catch on, like.

BAZOOKA JOE

It says '200 Dead Up Redruth Cemetery'.

HEDLEY

Thanks very much, says I, an' goes on my way, calling out the news from the *Cornish Evening Tidings*. 200 Dead Up Redruth Cemetery!

FIRST VOICE

At this, and no matter how many

times he told them, the boys would be rolling in the gutter with laughter and delight. But Hedley paid them no heed, and carried on with his tale, with almost childlike diligence.

HEDLEY

Well, I encountered many happy faces that day, I can tell ee, an' sold out o' papers 'fore I even got to the bottom of West End. Nex' day I seen ol' Ernie Quick. 'What 'a say Ernie?' Well, people was fast to catch on, and Ernie was no exception.

ERNIE QUICK

Hitler Shit Hisself.

HEDLEY

Says Ernie, quick as you like. So there's me stanking round the town, crying 'Hitler Shit Hisself, Hitler Shit Hisself' an' looking like a g'eat wassack. Can't think 'ow I dedn' catch on, mind.

FIRST VOICE

By now point the boys would be dying of laughter, with Hedley shaking his head as he got up to leave. Hoisting his bag over his shoulder, his parting shot might be...

HEDLEY

'Ere, ded I ever tell ee 'bout the time some bugger 'ad me 'ollerin' 'Last Chance To Enter Miss Cornwall'?

❧ GRIZZLING ❧

CHUFFA

'Ere, you lot, you reckon Hedley Headlines can holler loud, eh? Well get your ears ready for this... I'M STILL LOST!

FIRST VOICE

Oh Chuffa, just hang on a bit will you? We'll get there, don't you worry.

CHUFFA

Well just mind you do... or else I'll just have to go off and find myself.

FIRST VOICE

Go on Eli.

LITTLE ELI

At other times we had loads to choose from if we felt like a good grizzle. We might run away from Johnny Bash, who would sit evening after evening with his fists in a bucket of brine...

JOHNNY BASH

To make'n 'ard.

BILLY OUGH

Then there was Dr Tregarthen, whose housekeeper boiled up rat and served it to him as chicken after he scolded her for nothing – and he never even suspected.

JACEY BLIMMER

Old Mrs Glink, who always carried round two cardboard suitcases full of nothing.

DAVY ISAACS

Jabby Joan, who pocked her flesh with blackthorns 'til it bled.

DICKY DIDO

Grooter Smale, who some said had worn the same set of clothes for fifty year.

JACK TUSSER

And Jim Spratt, who was so ancient that even the old folk of the parish were sure he'd been the same age as their grandparents when they were children.

LITTLE ELI

But this was Christmas, and none of our usual victims seemed to have been allowed out. So we had to rely on our own for amusement.

CHUFFA

That's where I come in.

FIRST VOICE

That's right, Chuffa, I said we'd get to you.

CHUFFA

You goin' find me now?

JACK TUSSER

It was me that found him.

FIRST VOICE

That's right, Jack.

JACK TUSSER

But if I'd known he was goin' be this much trouble I wouldn't have bothered.

FIRST VOICE

What Chuffa had not bargained for, when he crept into the empty *Sweet & Golden* crate, were the bustlings of Bessie Bubby, who thought she would have...

AUNTIE BESSY BUBBY

A bit of a tidy up to help out, like.

FIRST VOICE

And dragged the box half a mile down the track to the dustbins.

BILLY OUGH

Chuffa was still sleeping when Jack found him three whole hours later.

CHUFFA

About time too, I was bleddy freezin' and hungry. Where's my old box? I want my own box back. Some bleddy Christmas this has turned out to be.

GRANFER

LITTLE ELI

Then there was the terrible
Christmas when Granfer just got up
from his tea and died. The sun, around
which we had all orbited, shone no
more; the harbour we all sought in
stormy times, put up its blocks for ever
and was swept away. And when he died,
we cried torrents of tears which washed
away so many Christmases to come. Our
tears swept away the decorations, the
fairy lights, baubles and streamers; greet-
ings cards with sobbing Santas turned to
pulp, the snowmen figures on the uncut
Christmas cake bowed their little pom-
pomed heads; for they knew, as we knew,
and as Granfer surely knew, we could
never return to those Christmases of

old. And when we children were ushered outside, our smudged and smarted eyes averted, as if this man we had loved and laughed with only moments before was somehow no longer to be gazed upon or cuddled, our tears ran down our faces and dripped off our noses, dissolving in the sleety puddles at our feet, to run into the river, passing under the little coombe bridges to the bone yard, and there, mingled, salt on salt, in the Atlantic.

DICKY DIDO

Where will they bury your granfer?

FIRST VOICE

Asked Dicky Dido cheerfully the following morning.

DICKY DIDO

Churchyard? Or at sea like a pirate?

JACK TUSSER

They won't get me up no churchyard.

Too much effing religion, my Da says.
My Da says all that God and Jesus stuff
never done no one no good. Better be a
'eathen any day, you.

ꙮ Tissue Paper ꙮ

FIRST VOICE

That's a point – where *were* God and Jesus and all the angels in all of this?

DICKY DIDO

Well, they were there all right, but usually didn't turn up until after tea, when the singing began.

LITTLE ELI

Always we would sing.

FIRST VOICE

Badly, nervously, self-consciously at first, then with passion and gusto, full of cheers and tears. Strange, unfathomable songs like...

ALL

Ee saw I an' I saw ee an' ee was up yon wurzel tree, with a bloody g'eat stick I'll 'ammer ee, blackbird I'll 'ave ee.

FIRST VOICE

And...

ALL

The hairs on 'er dicky dido hung down to
'er knees.

FIRST VOICE

And...

ALL

Tissue paper, tissue paper, marmalade or
jam.

FIRST VOICE

And...

ALL

Well, Hello Dolly!

JIMMY JAMPOT

Pentreath!

ALL

Well, Hello Dolly!

JIMMY JAMPOT

Pentreath!

ALL

It's some nice to 'ave ee back where you d'belong.

JIMMY JAMPOT

Up Paul!

FIRST VOICE

Glorious songs like...

ALL

I love the white rose in its splendour, I love the white rose in its bloom, I love the white rose, so fair as she grows, it's the rose that reminds me of you.

FIRST VOICE

And...

ALL

Her eyes they shone like diamonds and the evening it was wet wet wet.

FIRST VOICE

And...

ALL

Hail to the Homeland, great bastion of the free, hear now thy children, proclaim their love for thee, ageless thy splendour, undimmed the Celtic flame, proudly our souls reflect the glory of thy name.

FIRST VOICE

Sacred songs like...

ALL

Then sings my soul, my saviour God to thee, how great thou art, how great thou art.

FIRST VOICE

And...

ALL

Immortal, invisible, God only wise, in light inaccessible, hid from our eyes.

FIRST VOICE

Or...

ALL

Oh come, oh come, Emmanuel, and ransom captive Israel, that mourns in lonely exile here, until the Son of God appear.

FIRST VOICE

And...

ALL

All night, all night, the angels are watching o'er me, all night, all night, the angels are watching o'er me.

FIRST VOICE

And...

ALL

We'll never say goodbye, we'll never say goodbye, for in that land of joy and song, we'll never say goodbye.

❧ GOD ❧

LITTLE ELI

Last thing on Christmas Night – mizzle or no – we children would all be sent away up the dancers, so the adults could drink the last of the brown ale, advocaat and *Sweet & Golden*, nibble at nuts and dates, play some cards and idle in a fug of excess. Only then did Uncle Artie stir. Quietly he would climb the Timbern Hill, sit on the end of one of the big beds and tell us his favourite story of when God created the world.

UNCLE ARTIE

After fashioning all the marvellous lands from Algeria to Zimbabwe, Aruba to Zanzibar, and dividing them up amongst the peoples of the world, God lay down to rest. But just as he was about to fall into a deep and satisfied sleep, knowing there was no more work to do, there came a light knock at his door. On enquiring who would disturb God after his magnificent labours, he heard a small, but familiar voice.

VOICE OF THE CORNISH

'Tes us, Lord. The Cornish.

GOD

Well, what do you want at this hour? I've had quite a hard day creating the world. I need to sleep.

VOICE OF THE CORNISH

Well, 'tes like this, see. We abn' got nowhere to live – there's nowhere left.

GOD

Weren't you here earlier? Did I not allocate you a homeland like everyone else?

VOICE OF THE CORNISH

Well God, it was like this, see, we

meant to turn up at the time you said,
but then we thought, well, we don't want
to be too pushy like, an' there was a long
line of other folk, an' there dedn' seem
no need for no urgency in the matter, so
we thought we'd leave everyone else
queue up first an' spake to ee later.

GOD

This is most troubling.

UNCLE ARTIE

Said God, rising from his bed.

GOD

Thing is, I haven't got nothing left.

VOICE OF THE CORNISH

Gar! What am I goin' tell the missus?

GOD

Tell ee what.

UNCLE ARTIE

Continued God.

GOD

There is one place, but–

VOICE OF THE CORNISH

We'll abn! Don't madder what 'tes like, lumpy or flat, boggy or parched, 'igh or low, uplong, downlong, backlong, we'll take'n.

GOD

Awright, awright, hauld tongue will ee. I need to think.

VOICE OF THE CORNISH

Sorry God, but you knaw 'ow 'tes – my missus'll lace me if I don't come back with a lil' splat.

GOD

Thing is, I was planning on keeping it back for myself.

VOICE OF THE CORNISH

Well, where is 'a azackly?

UNCLE ARTIE

God pointed his long bony finger.

GOD

See down there, that lil' small place,

shaped a bit like a bulging Christmas stocking?

VOICE OF THE CORNISH

What, there, jus' to the bottom left of the British Isles, all clothed in mizzle?

GOD

The very one. As I say, I was planning on settling there myself, but I suppose... we can share 'en.

LITTLE ELI

And so, sleep swept over us as another Christmas Night came to a close and we settled our fortunately childish heads on soft pillows in a little house on the side of the Hill of Wonder in...

ALL

God's Own Country.

✿ THE WRITER ✿

Simon Parker's work includes *Full As An Egg* (Truran 2006), *Chasing Tales – The Lost Stories Of Charles Lee* and *A Star On The Mizzen*. It has been performed on BBC Radio 4, BBC Radio Cornwall and by Kneehigh Theatre and Sterts Theatre. A founder member of *Scavel An Gow*, editor of *Scryfa* and a Bard of the Cornish Gorsedd (*Scryfer Carn Marth*), he works as a writer and editor for *The Western Morning News* and lives with his wife and three children on the edge of Bodmin Moor in Cornwall.

❧ THE ARTIST ❧

Clive Wakfer is a professional cartoonist and illustrator. Born in Cornwall, he was inspired by drawings in comics and annuals. He attended Somerset College of Art, and had his first exhibition in Bristol. His work appears in books, magazines, newspapers, advertising and even on carpets and thimbles. He lists his best achievements as "my children, a black belt in karate and meeting Norman Wisdom on Newlyn Green". He can be contacted at: clivewakfer@melvia.fsnet.co.uk